THE NHL: HISTORY AND HEROES

BOSTON
BRUINS

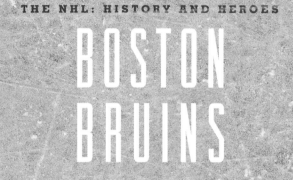

JOHN NICHOLS

E NHL: HISTORY AND HEROES

Published by Creative Education
P.O. Box 227, Mankato, Minnesota 56002
Creative Education is an imprint of The Creative Company.

DESIGN AND PRODUCTION BY **ZENO DESIGN**

Printed in the United States of America

PHOTOGRAPHS BY Corbis (Bettmann, Louie Psihoyos), Getty Images (Brian Babineau/SA,
Steve Babineau/SA, Bruce Bennett Studios, Focus on Sport, FPG, Vito Palmisano, Andre
Pichette, Dave Sandford, Ezra Shaw/Allsport)

LIBRARY OF CONGRESS CATALOGING-IN-PUBLICATION DATA

Nichols, John, 1966–
The story of the Boston Bruins / by John Nichols.
p. cm. — (The NHL: history and heroes)
Includes index
ISBN 978-1-58341-614-3
1. Boston Bruins (Hockey team)—History. 2. Hockey teams—United States—History. I. Title.
II. Series.

GV848.B6N54 2008
796.962'640974461—dc22   2007014997

First Edition

9 8 7 6 5 4 3 2 1

COVER: Center Marc Savard

BOSTON
BRUINS

IT WAS OVERTIME, AND THE BOSTON GARDEN CROWD WAS ON ITS FEET. ONE MORE GOAL AND THE HOMETOWN BOSTON BRUINS WOULD CLINCH THEIR FIRST WORLD CHAMPIONSHIP IN NEARLY 30 YEARS. A ROAR BEGAN TO BUILD IN THE ARENA AS A BROAD-SHOULDERED MAN WEARING THE HOME TEAM'S NUMBER 4 SWEATER CORRALLED A LOOSE PUCK ALONG THE RIGHT BOARDS. THE FANS HAD SEEN MANY TIMES BEFORE WHAT BOBBY ORR WAS ABOUT TO DO, BUT IT NEVER CEASED TO AMAZE THEM. AFTER WHIPPING A QUICK PASS TO A TEAMMATE BEHIND THE

BRUINS

OPPOSING GOAL, ORR SWOOPED TOWARD THE NET, GATHERED IN A RETURN PASS, AND DEFTLY SNAPPED THE PUCK PAST ST. LOUIS BLUES GOALIE GLENN HALL. TRIPPED BY A TRAILING DEFENDER AND SENT AIRBORNE, ARMS OUTSTRETCHED, ORR APPEARED TO FLY LIKE THE HOCKEY SUPERMAN HE WAS AS THE PUCK FOUND THE NET. THE BOSTON BRUINS WERE THE 1970 STANLEY CUP CHAMPIONS, AND BOBBY ORR WAS HOCKEY'S BIGGEST STAR.

THE BABY BRUINS

THE CITY OF BOSTON IS THE CAPITAL OF Massachusetts. Located in America's New England region, Boston is a bustling harbor town with a rich history that dates back to the days of the American Revolution. It was here that Paul Revere made his famous midnight ride, and modern Boston is home to many of the nation's oldest and finest educational, financial, cultural, and medical centers.

Founded nearly 400 years ago, Boston was the site of some of America's earliest developments in shipping, education, and professional sports.

Boston is also famous for its love of sports, and one of the professional teams Boston sports fans hold most dear is the National Hockey League's (NHL) Boston Bruins. Founded in 1924, the franchise drew its name from a contest in which entries were to relate to an untamed animal of "size, strength, agility, ferocity, and cunning." The Bruins—another word for bears—have been prowling the ranks of the NHL ever since.

In 1924–25, the NHL consisted of only six teams: the Boston Bruins, Hamilton Tigers, Montreal Canadiens, Montreal Maroons, Ottawa Senators, and Toronto St. Patricks. The first edition of the Bruins won only 6 of 30 games in 1924–25. But what the Bruins lacked in talent, they made up for in leadership. Head coach and general manager Art Ross quickly established himself as one of the top minds in the game. Over the next 30 years, Ross would mold the Bruins into a tough and fiercely competitive franchise. Ross's impact on the game would be so great that the NHL would name its trophy for the league's leading point scorer after him.

One of Ross's best early moves was signing a bruising young defenseman by the name of Eddie Shore. The 5-foot-11 (175 cm) and 190-pound (86 kg) Shore debuted in 1926 and immediately improved Boston's fortunes. Shore's swift skating, uncanny passing ability, and fearsome body checking made him the Bruins' first true star. "Shore plays like someone on the other team stole something from him," said Bruins wing Harry Oliver. "He leaves bruises."

Early Bruins great Eddie Shore won the Hart Trophy as the NHL's Most Valuable Player four times—a record for defensemen that still stands.

As the 1920s wore on, Boston continued to improve. Along with Shore, the Bruins featured such standouts as centers Ralph "Cooney" Weiland and Norman "Dutch" Gainor and winger Aubrey "Dit" Clapper. Together, Weiland, Gainor, and Clapper formed a goal-scoring unit so explosive that it became known as the "Dynamite Line." Led by Shore and the Dynamite Line, the 1928–29 Bruins captured the American Division title. In the playoffs, Boston stormed past the Montreal Canadiens and the New York Rangers to capture the NHL championship and the Stanley Cup—the silver chalice that is hockey's most valued prize.

Boston remained a strong team throughout the 1930s but struggled in the playoffs. The Bruins' potent offense, featuring forwards Milt Schmidt, Woody Dumart, and Bobby Bauer, helped the team finish first or second in its division seven times between 1930 and 1938, good enough to earn a spot in the

Phil Esposito CENTER

Esposito was neither a fast nor a graceful skater. But what he could do better than anyone who ever played was anchor his powerful body in front of the opposing goal and snap loose pucks into the net. Esposito was strong and gifted with great hand-eye coordination, and no rebound was safe with him around. A popular saying in Boston at the time was, "Jesus saves, Espo scores on the rebound." A charismatic and vocal leader, Esposito loved to keep his teammates loose by playing practical jokes on them. "If you found something strange in your locker, you knew you had Espo to thank," said defenseman Gary Doak.

BRUINS SEASONS: 1967–76
HEIGHT: 6-1 (185 cm)
WEIGHT: 205 (93 kg)

- 2-time Hart Trophy winner (as league MVP)
- 717 career goals
- 5-time Ross Trophy winner (as NHL points leader)
- Hockey Hall of Fame inductee (1984)

High-scoring center Milt Schmidt, who would later coach the Bruins for a decade, played with a reckless style that left him frequently injured.

postseason. But each hopeful playoff appearance ended in disappointment, as the Bruins were knocked out every time. Finally, in 1939, the Bruins ended their playoff frustration by defeating the Toronto Maple Leafs and capturing the Stanley Cup for the second time.

The unexpected star of that 1938–39 season was rookie goalie Frank Brimsek. Brimsek was thrust into the spotlight when the Bruins traded star goalie Cecil "Tiny" Thompson to the Detroit Red Wings early in the season. Brimsek rewarded the team's faith in him by posting 10 shutouts and a 1.57 goals against average (GAA), numbers that earned him the Calder Trophy as the league's Rookie of the Year and the Vezina Trophy as the NHL's top goalie. Brimsek was so dominant that his teammates nicknamed him "Mr. Zero."

"To be a great goalie, you have to be quick, have good eyes, and it helps to be either really brave or really crazy."

BOSTON GOALIE FRANK BRIMSEK

12

BRUINS

The Glorious Garden

FOR 67 YEARS, THE BOSTON BRUINS knew only one home—the Boston Garden. The "Gahden," as it was called by the Boston faithful, was built in 1928 as a venue for boxing, and its seating put fans much closer to the action than most arenas. Passionate Bruins fans filled the Garden with noise, and the rink's smaller ice surface (the Garden could accommodate a rink length of only 185 feet (56 m)—15 feet (4.5 m) shorter than standard NHL rinks) continually threw opponents off their game. As much as Boston fans loved the Garden, opponents hated it. Visiting teams frequently complained about the Garden's tiny locker room, cold-water showers, and lack of working plumbing. From 1928 to 1995, the Bruins brought five Stanley Cup championships and 22 division titles home to their beloved arena. But eventually, the Garden began to show its age. The arena's lack of air conditioning and balky electrical system contributed to power outages that marred the Bruins' Stanley Cup Finals appearances in 1988 and 1990. In 1995, the team moved to a new arena, the FleetCenter (now called the TD Banknorth Garden), and the Boston Garden was torn down. The "Gahden" may be gone, but Boston fans will never forget it.

FROM SHORE TO BUCYK

DURING THE 1939–40 SEASON, AN ERA OF Bruins hockey came to an end when Eddie Shore was traded to the New York Americans. But even without its former star, Boston put together an impressive 27–8–13 record in 1940–41. Center Bill Cowley was the team's spark plug. He led the league in scoring with 62 points (goals plus assists) and won the Hart Trophy as the league's Most Valuable Player (MVP). The Bruins were flat-out dominant during the regular season, setting an NHL record by going 23 games without a loss. In the playoffs, Boston showed great character in overcoming a three-games-to-two deficit to defeat Toronto in seven games. Then, in the Stanley Cup Finals, Boston steamrolled the Detroit Red Wings in four straight games, becoming the first team ever to execute a four-game Finals sweep.

Frank Brimsek, who was famously cool in clutch situations, won eight games and lost just three in the 1941 playoffs, giving Boston the Stanley Cup.

For the next two decades, Boston remained a contender, making the Stanley Cup Finals five more times during the 1940s and '50s. High-scoring players such as center Fleming Mackell and right wing John Peirson kept the Bruins in the hunt for the Cup almost every year. But each time Boston made the Finals, it came up short. The Bruins' biggest nemesis during these years was the Montreal Canadiens. The powerful Canadiens denied Boston the Cup in 1946, 1953, 1957, and 1958. "We had some mighty fine clubs during the '50s," said hard-charging wing Leo LaBine. "But no matter how good we were, Montreal was always just a little bit better."

As the 1950s ended, so did Boston's long stretch of winning hockey. The Bruins' older stars could no longer carry the load, and the team's minor-league system was unable to produce quality players to replace them. From 1960 to 1967, the Bruins posted eight straight losing seasons. But even during

Johnny Bucyk WING

A star player into his 40s, Johnny Bucyk made many Bruins fans wonder if he could play forever. During his 21 seasons in Boston, Bucyk was the model of consistency and durability. He scored 20 or more goals in 16 seasons, and in 1971, at age 35, he became the oldest player in NHL history to score 50 goals in a season. Nicknamed "The Chief" after a sportswriter once mistook him for a native Canadian because of his dark features, Bucyk led Boston with uncompromising character. Despite being known for his fearsome hip checks, Bucyk twice won the Lady Byng Trophy for his sportsmanship and gentlemanly play.

BRUINS SEASONS: 1957–78
HEIGHT: 6-0 (183 cm)
WEIGHT: 215 (97.5 kg)

- 556 career goals
- 813 career assists
- 7-time All-Star
- Hockey Hall of Fame inductee (1981)

Hall of Fame goalie Terry Sawchuk spent most of his career with the Detroit Red Wings but starred in a Bruins sweater in 1955–56 and 1956–57.

these dark times, Bruins fans came out in droves to support their team. In fact, the losing Bruins consistently drew larger crowds to their home arena, the Boston Garden, than did the Boston Celtics, who won multiple National Basketball Association (NBA) championships in the 1960s.

"Through the tough years, I dreamed this day would come. Today I got to hold up the Stanley Cup. Man, it was worth it. It was worth it."

BOSTON WING JOHNNY BUCYK,
ON WINNING THE 1970 STANLEY CUP

One of the reasons Bruins fans kept coming out was the play of left wing Johnny Bucyk. Bucyk wore the number 9 Boston sweater from 1957 to 1978. The rugged, 6-foot (183 cm) and 215-pounder (97.5 kg) scored 545 goals during his Bruins career (the most in club history) and kept hope alive during the bleak seasons. "John worked harder and gave more to this organization than anybody will ever know," said wing Ken Hodge, a longtime teammate. "John *is* Boston Bruins hockey."

18

BRUINS

Willie O'Ree: Hockey Pioneer

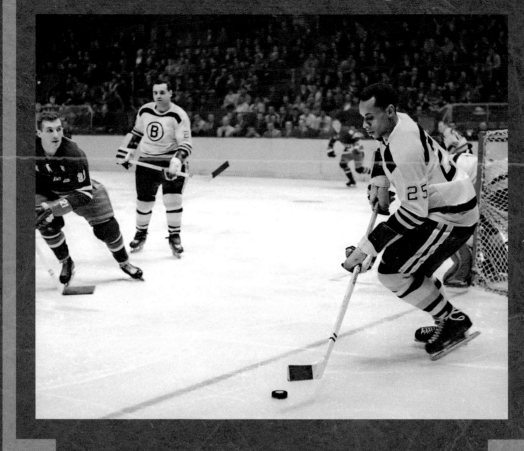

WILLIE O'REE'S NHL CAREER LASTED fewer than 50 games, but his contribution to the sport is still felt today. On January 18, 1958, O'Ree became the first black player in the history of the NHL when he skated for the Bruins against the Montreal Canadiens. The event was little-noted at the time, as O'Ree played only two midseason games before being sent back down to the minor leagues. But during the 1960–61 season, O'Ree returned to the Bruins and played 43 games, scoring 4 goals and notching 10 assists. He would never play in the NHL again after that season, but the fact that he played at all was a major accomplishment. In addition to the racial prejudice he encountered, O'Ree was nearly blind in his right eye, the result of being hit by a puck two years before his NHL debut. O'Ree played on despite his injury and was a solid winger known for his speed and good body checking. After O'Ree's brief career, it would be 14 years before another black player would appear in an NHL game, but O'Ree's accomplishment paved the way for later black stars such as Calgary Flames wing Jarome Iginla and Edmonton Oilers goaltender Grant Fuhr.

ORR AND ESPO LEAD THE WAY

BOSTON'S LOSING RUN ENDED WHEN THE team signed an 18-year-old defenseman by the name of Bobby Orr. The strapping youngster came into the league in 1966 heralded as the NHL's next big star, and his dazzling combination of stickhandling and creativity redefined modern hockey. Before Orr came along, defensemen rarely strayed far from their own net and contributed little offensively. But Orr's explosive speed and great agility allowed him to venture deep into enemy territory and create scoring chances. In 1966–67, Orr scored 41 points in 61 games and won the Calder Trophy. "Many times I saw Bobby carry the puck from behind his own net, weave through about three or four guys, get a hard shot on goal, and then—*boom*—he'd beat the other team back down the ice before they could get a rush going," said Bruins wing Wayne Cashman.

20

BRUINS

Although his career was cut short by knee injuries, defenseman extraordinaire Bobby Orr captivated Boston crowds for 10 seasons with his rare speed.

As the 1960s wore on, the Bruins built a winner around their boy-wonder defenseman and the veteran Bucyk. Stars such as Hodge and high-scoring center Phil Esposito were also acquired via trades. Cashman and Don Marcotte provided scoring punch from the wings, Gerry Cheevers developed into a top goaltender, and flashy center Derek Sanderson followed Orr as the Calder Trophy winner in 1968. This collection of hard-charging stars propelled the Bruins back into championship contention.

In 1969–70, behind Orr's 120 points and Esposito's 43 goals, Boston romped through the regular season. In the playoffs, the Bruins quickly dispatched New York and Chicago to set up a Stanley Cup Finals showdown with the St. Louis Blues. Boston easily won the first three games of the series, but in Game 4, played in Boston, St. Louis held a 3–2 lead in the third period. With time running out, Bucyk netted the tying goal, sending the game into sudden-death

Terry O'Reilly WING

Fierce, scrappy, and aggressive, O'Reilly was the engine that powered the blue-collar Bruins of the late 1970s. O'Reilly did not possess the talent of many other stars, but he made up for it with sheer determination. The winger was wildly popular among Boston's large Irish population and was known for doing whatever it took to motivate his team—whether that was scoring a goal, blocking a shot with his body, or fighting. No stranger to the "sin bin," at the 2002 ceremony held to retire his number 24 sweater, O'Reilly waved to the Boston faithful and then delighted them by taking a seat in the penalty box.

BRUINS SEASONS: 1971–85
HEIGHT: 6-1 (185 cm)
WEIGHT: 200 (91 kg)

- 204 career goals
- 2-time All-Star
- 2,095 career penalty minutes
- 402 career assists

Phil Esposito (right) was famous for his ability to plant himself in front of the opposing goal, wait for rebounds, and stuff them back into the net.

overtime. Early in overtime, Orr joined a Boston rush. Zipping past a defender, the fleet defenseman streaked toward the St. Louis goal and snapped a perfect Sanderson pass into the net. The series was over, and the Bruins were Stanley Cup champions for the first time since 1941.

With all of its young stars returning, Boston was favored to repeat as champion in 1970–71. The combination of Orr and Esposito gave the team a one-two scoring punch the likes of which had never been seen before in the NHL. During the 1970–71 season, Esposito netted a league-record 76 goals and added 76 assists for another NHL record of 152 points. Orr, meanwhile, notched 37 goals and 102 assists for a total of 139 points. So powerful was the team's offense that six of the top eight scorers in the NHL that season wore Boston black and gold. The Bruins juggernaut rolled to the playoffs, but in a shocking first-round upset, Boston's old nemesis, the Montreal Canadiens, defeated the Bruins in seven hard-fought games.

Motivated by the defeat, Boston came back the next year determined to reclaim its place atop the NHL. The "Big Bad Bruins" rolled to a 54–13–11 regular-season record. In the postseason, Boston's dominance continued as the Bruins battled past Toronto, St. Louis, and New York on their way to a fifth Stanley Cup championship.

24

BRUINS

Man Behind the Mask

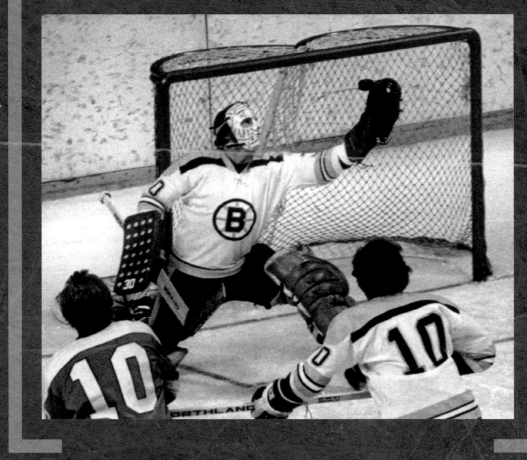

DURING THE 1971–72 SEASON, BRUINS goalie Gerry Cheevers was nearly invincible. The charismatic netminder set an NHL record by going 32 games (24 victories and 8 ties) without a loss. Cheevers's incredible feat helped cement his reputation as a "money" goaltender—at his best when the stakes were the highest. With him in net, the Bruins won Stanley Cup titles in 1970 and 1972. Far from a traditional "stand-up" goalie, Cheevers would flop wildly on the ice using any part of his body to stop shots. He was also famous for his mask. One day in practice, a puck struck Cheevers in the formfitted mask. After going to the locker room to recover, Cheevers returned to the ice, but as a joke, the Bruins' trainer had painted surgical stitches on the mask where he had been hit. From then on, every time Cheevers was hit in the mask with a shot, the trainer would paint new stitches on his mask. By the end of his career, Cheevers's mask was covered in stitches and had become one of the most recognizable images in the game. The mask can today be seen in the Hockey Hall of Fame in Toronto, Ontario.

BLUE-COLLAR BRUINS

BOSTON CONTINUED TO RIDE THE STRONG
shoulders of Orr and Esposito until the 1975–76 season, when crippling knee injuries sidelined Orr, and
Esposito was traded to New York for defenseman
Brad Park and center Jean Ratelle. Orr would never
be the same, sitting out a season and then retiring
after a brief comeback with the Chicago Blackhawks.
Between them, Orr and Esposito had captured the
Hart Trophy five times and the Ross Trophy seven
times during their reign in Boston.

"Well the first thing, when I saw Orr
coming down on me, was to say a
little prayer, if I had time."

TORONTO MAPLE LEAFS GOALIE JOHNNY BOWER,
ON STOPPING BOBBY ORR

BRUINS

One of the NHL's finest defenders of the 1970s and '80s, Brad Park never won the Norris Trophy but was runner-up a league-record six times.

Without their two marquee stars, the Bruins found a different way to win. Fiery new coach Don Cherry preached a blue-collar style that emphasized hustle, body checking, and hard work. The club's new leader on the ice was Terry O'Reilly. The 6-foot-1 (185 cm) and 200-pound (91 kg) wing was an immediate fan favorite, and his intense, brawling style often overshadowed his solid goal-scoring skills.

During the 1977–78 season, O'Reilly became the first player in NHL history to log 200 or more penalty minutes while also finishing among the league's top 10 scorers. O'Reilly and defenseman Mike Milbury provided the grit for the Bruins' success in the late 1970s, while Park, Ratelle, and winger Rick Middleton provided the polish. "We were quite a bunch," said Milbury. "Even if we didn't beat you on the scoreboard, you'd leave the arena with enough bruises to feel like you'd lost."

BRUINS ALL-TIME TEAM

Bobby Orr DEFENSEMAN

Widely regarded as the best defenseman ever to play the game, Orr revolutionized the position with his speed, playmaking, and vision. In an era when defensemen rarely joined the offensive rush, Orr's jaw-dropping, end-to-end charges dazzled both defenders and fans. In addition to his offensive prowess, Orr was a stout defender and a bruising physical presence. Despite having his career shortened by knee injuries, Orr completely rewrote the league record book for defensemen. His 1974–75 season, in which he scored 46 goals and notched 89 assists, is generally considered the greatest season ever assembled by a defenseman.

BRUINS SEASONS: 1966–76
HEIGHT: 6-0 (183 cm)
WEIGHT: 200 (91 kg)

- 8-time Norris Trophy winner (as best defenseman)
- 3-time Hart Trophy winner
- 1967 Calder Trophy winner (as Rookie of the Year)
- Hockey Hall of Fame inductee (1979)

Known for his love of physical play, Don Cherry assembled an impressive 231–105–64 regular-season record during his five years as Boston's coach.

29

BRUINS

The Bruins reached the Stanley Cup Finals twice during Cherry's tenure as head coach. Unfortunately for Boston fans, the scrappy Bruins were defeated each time, getting swept in four games by Montreal in 1977 and going six games before bowing to the Canadiens again in 1978. The Bruins of the 1970s would get one more crack at solving the Montreal playoff riddle in 1979. This time the two rivals met in the Stanley Cup semifinals.

> "My guys can't skate too good, aren't real cute with the puck, and can't shoot their way out of a wet paper bag, but we'll work you to death. That, I can promise you."
>
> BOSTON COACH DON CHERRY

After the teams split the first six games, the Bruins were on the verge of victory in Game 7 as they led 4–3 with time running out. But a late penalty for too many men on the ice let Montreal score the tying goal and force overtime. The Canadiens then scored again in overtime to deliver another crushing playoff defeat to the Bruins. Cherry then left the team for a career in broadcasting. As the hot-blooded coach vacated the stage, another Bruins great was about to enter.

30

BRUINS

"Bep" Brings Youthful Pep

AT AGE 16, MOST TEENAGE BOYS are just figuring out high school. Not so with Armand "Bep" Guidolin. On November 12, 1942, the talented teenager became the youngest player ever in the NHL (16 years, 11 months, and 27 days). The 5-foot-8 (173 cm) and 175-pound (79 kg) youngster's path to the NHL was sped by his talent and the fact that the Bruins were in dire need of replacements for players who had left to fight in World War II. Guidolin, a left wing, tallied 24 and 40 points (in 50-game seasons) during his first two campaigns with the Bruins. In 1944, he became old enough to join the armed forces and left to serve in the war. After the war, he returned to the Bruins. Many thought he would struggle against the returned NHL regulars, but Guidolin proved to be a solid player in the league for seven more seasons. Guidolin had been nicknamed "Bep" by his Italian-speaking mother, and the name stuck, as hockey broadcaster Foster Hewitt feared tangling his tongue around Guidolin's birth name. After his playing career ended, Guidolin enjoyed a long coaching career and eventually served as head coach of the Bruins in the 1970s. "My story is every boy's dream," said Guidolin.

A RAY OF LIGHT

BOSTON'S LONG HISTORY OF GREAT DEFENSEMEN continued when the team drafted Ray Bourque with its first-round pick in the 1979 NHL Draft. Like Shore and Orr before him, Bourque made an immediate impact, scoring 65 points in 1979–80 and winning the Calder Trophy. Also like his famous predecessors, Bourque possessed rare offensive skills while sacrificing nothing on defense. His speed, strength, and uncommonly hard shot complemented a deep understanding of the game. "You never catch Ray out of position," noted Bruins goalie Andy Moog. "He anticipates everything so well, it's almost like he knows what you are going to do before you do."

Rarely flashy but always quietly brilliant, Ray Bourque captained the Bruins for 12 seasons and played in a Boston-record 1,518 total games.

Along with his many talents, Bourque also displayed iron-man consistency. He would play for 21 seasons in Boston and make the All-Star team 18 times. During his career, he would play alongside such Bruins as Terry O'Reilly in the '70s, center Barry Pederson in the '80s, wing Cam Neely in the '90s, and center Joe Thornton at the dawn of the 21st century. While all would leave their mark on Bruins history, Bourque was the tie that bound them together.

The pinnacle of the Bourque era came during the late 1980s and early '90s, when Bourque and the high-scoring Neely spurred the Bruins to the Stanley Cup Finals twice. In 1988, the Bruins posted a 44–30–6 record and defeated the Buffalo Sabres in the first round of the playoffs. In the second round, Boston faced its old rival, the Montreal Canadiens, but this time the Bruins prevailed, knocking Montreal out in five games. The victory marked the first time Boston had defeated Montreal in the playoffs in 45 years. Riding

Ray Bourque DEFENSEMAN

Through 21 seasons with the Bruins, Ray Bourque personified quiet excellence. Rock-steady on defense and uniquely gifted on offense, Bourque made the incredible seem ordinary every time he took the ice. Bourque burst onto the NHL scene in 1979. The 19-year-old made history when he won the Calder Trophy as Rookie of the Year and became the first non-goalie rookie to be named a First-Team All-Star. Bruins fans could always rely on the rarely injured Bourque's laser-like slap shot and booming checks. At the conclusion of his career, Bourque stood as the NHL's all-time leading scorer among defensemen.

BRUINS SEASONS: 1979–2000
HEIGHT: 6-0 (183 cm)
WEIGHT: 219 (99 kg)

- 18-time All-Star
- 410 career goals
- 5-time Norris Trophy winner
- Hockey Hall of Fame inductee (2004)

Cam Neely did it all for the Bruins, delivering teeth-rattling body checks and leading the team in goals for five straight seasons in the late '80s.

the momentum of the Montreal victory, the Bruins dispatched the New Jersey Devils in the Wales Conference Finals en route to a championship matchup with the Edmonton Oilers. The Bruins played their hearts out but were swept by the powerful Oilers and their star center, Wayne Gretzky, in four games.

In 1989–90, the Bruins' stingy defense, led by Moog and fellow goalie Reggie Lemelin, allowed the fewest goals in the league. On the offensive side, Neely and Bourque again led the charge, as the bruising winger and speedy defenseman combined for 176 points. In the playoffs, Boston steamed past the Hartford Whalers, Montreal Canadiens, and Washington Capitals on their way to a Stanley Cup Finals rematch with Edmonton.

"I heard a lot of Ray Bourque's shots, but I didn't see hardly any of them."

WASHINGTON CAPITALS GOALIE
CLINT MALARCHUK

The series seemed to turn on Game 1, when the defense-minded Bruins battled the high-scoring Oilers to three overtimes before losing 3–2. The Bruins never recovered from the draining defeat and lost the series in five games. "Hockey is a funny game," Neely said sadly after the series. "The puck bounces a different way in Game 1 and maybe it's us holding up the Cup right now."

Boston remained a strong team throughout the mid-1990s, but as the decade drew to a close, so did the Bruins' remarkable run of winning hockey. Injuries, free agency, and age slowed the team. In 1996–97, Boston suffered a losing season for the first time in 30 years.

36

BRUINS

IN THE NEARLY 90-YEAR HISTORY of the Boston Bruins, some of the game's greatest players have worn the team's uniform. To honor the very best, the Bruins have retired the numbers of 11 players: numbers 2 (Eddie Shore), 3 (Lionel Hitchman), 4 (Bobby Orr), 5 (Dit Clapper), 7 (Phil Esposito), 8 (Cam Neely), 9 (Johnny Bucyk), 15 (Milt Schmidt), 24 (Terry O'Reilly), and 77 (Ray Bourque). Outside of these Bruins legends, the number 99 was retired league-wide by the NHL in 2000 to honor all-time great Wayne Gretzky, who never played for Boston. Today, Boston players and fans can look high in the rafters of the TD Banknorth Garden and see the banners bearing the numbers of the former Bruins stars and be reminded of the rich history that came before them. "When I got here in Boston, I was told you've got to have pride in that jersey," said Bourque on the 2001 night his number was retired. "Just watching that number go up and knowing it's going to be there in this building as long as it stands, that's quite a feeling."

BRINGING BACK THE GROWL

AS THE 1990S CAME TO AN END, THE BRUINS looked to rebuild their sagging franchise with young talent. High draft picks such as center Joe Thornton and winger Sergei Samsonov helped Boston get back on its feet. The 6-foot-4 (193 cm) and 210-pound (95 kg) Thornton brought a unique combination of power and skill, while the speedy Samsonov possessed a deft scoring touch and great playmaking vision. With the two young stars added to a lineup that still included Bourque and standout goalie Byron Dafoe, the Bruins began to improve.

Although small for an NHL player at just 5-foot-8 (173 cm), Sergei Samsonov used slick skating and stick-handling to become a key scorer and All-Star.

Boston made it back to the playoffs in 1998 and 1999, but while the team was good enough to make the postseason, it was still not talented enough to seriously compete for the Stanley Cup. With an eye to the future, Boston traded Bourque to the Colorado Avalanche late in the 1999–2000 season for younger talent.

After Bourque's departure, Boston fans looked to Thornton to become the next great Bruins star. Prior to the 2002–03 season, Thornton was named team captain, and he began to emerge as one of the league's premier players, notching 36 goals and 65 assists in 2002–03. The Bruins also got solid performances from veteran stars such as wingers Glen Murray and Mike Knuble. In 2003–04, the revitalized Bruins posted a 41–19–15 mark and captured the Eastern Conference's Northeast Division title. In the first round of the playoffs, Boston looked dominant as it jumped out to a three-games-to-one lead

Cecil "Tiny" Thompson GOALIE

Bruins fans knew from the beginning that Thompson was a special talent. In his first career start, he recorded a 1–0 shutout win versus the Pittsburgh Pirates. Despite his nickname, the 5-foot-11 (180 cm) Thompson was actually larger than most goalies of his era, and his game was bigger by far— during his 10-plus seasons in Boston, Thompson won the Vezina Trophy as the league's best goalie four times. Thompson also helped his team on the offensive end. During the 1935–36 season, Thompson became the first NHL goaltender ever to register an assist on a scoring play.

BRUINS SEASONS: 1928–39
HEIGHT: 5-11 (180 cm)
WEIGHT: 165 (75 kg)

- 74 career shutouts
- 284–194–75 career record
- 2.08 career goals against average (GGA)
- Hockey Hall of Fame inductee (1959)

The first overall pick of the 1997 NHL Draft, big center Joe Thornton experienced just one playoff series win during his eight seasons with the Bruins.

against Montreal. But then disaster struck as the Bruins dropped the next three games to lose the series to their longtime rivals. Unfortunately for Bruins fans, the painful memory of that loss lingered for a long time. The entire 2004–05 season was cancelled due to a lockout instituted by NHL owners after labor negotiations between owners and players collapsed.

After the owners and players finally worked out their differences, Boston hit the ice for the 2005–06 season looking to reestablish itself as a Stanley Cup contender. But the Bruins started slowly and by mid-year were in a tailspin that saw them lose 9 of 10 games. Desperate to get the team back on track, Boston dealt Thornton to the San Jose Sharks for winger Marco Sturm, center Wayne Primeau, and defenseman Brad Stuart. But the trade was unpopular among Boston fans and failed to spark the team. The Bruins limped to a 29–37–16 mark and missed the playoffs.

The Bruins entered the 2006–07 season with optimism. While the club focused on developing young talents such as center Patrice Bergeron, it also added key veterans such as huge defenseman Zdeno Chara and center Marc Savard. The 6-foot-9 (206 cm) and 265-pound (120 kg) Chara gave the Bruins an intimidating presence, while Savard's slick passing, leadership, and speed added needed punch to the Boston offense. The young Bruins finished 35–41–6 and out of the playoffs, but Boston was hopeful. "I like the nucleus of guys we've put together," said general manager Peter Chiarelli. "Boston deserves a winner, and I think we're putting together a team our fans can get behind."

42

BRUINS

Patrice Bergeron, a swift center with star potential, helped power the Bruins' scoring attack in 2006–07 by setting up Boston goals with 48 assists.

The Boston Bruins have a history of excellence that dates back to the birth of the NHL. For nearly nine decades, the Bruins have battled opponents with bear-like strength and ferocity, in the process producing some of the game's brightest stars and most thrilling moments. Having laid claim to five Stanley Cups and a deep roster of hockey greats, the Bruins plan to soon roar and make Boston the pro hockey capital of the world once again.

"If you play this game right, it's a thing of beauty. I like to think when we played, it was pretty to watch."

BOSTON WING BOBBY BAUER,
ON THE 1940S BRUINS

44

BRUINS

Bruins Ballet Fight Song

IT WOULD SEEM THAT THE BALLET is the last place a rough, tough professional hockey team would go to find its fight song. But that's exactly where the Boston Bruins found theirs. When a Boston television station began broadcasting Bruins games in the late 1960s, the station's managers wanted to come up with a suitable piece of music to air during the lead-in to each Bruins game. Because the city's ballet company was renowned for its annual holiday performance of the classic ballet *The Nutcracker*, the television station decided to go with an instrumental rock version of *The Nutcracker*'s overture, known as "Nutty" and performed by the band The Ventures. Nearly 40 years later, Nutty is still identified as the unofficial fight song of the Bruins. While the tune is not at all menacing nor especially inspirational, millions of Boston fans grew up knowing that when they heard Nutty, their Bruins heroes would soon be taking the ice. Nutty is still played during Bruins home games today, and Boston fans of all ages still cheer when the song's unforgettable, jaunty rhythm begins to course through the arena.

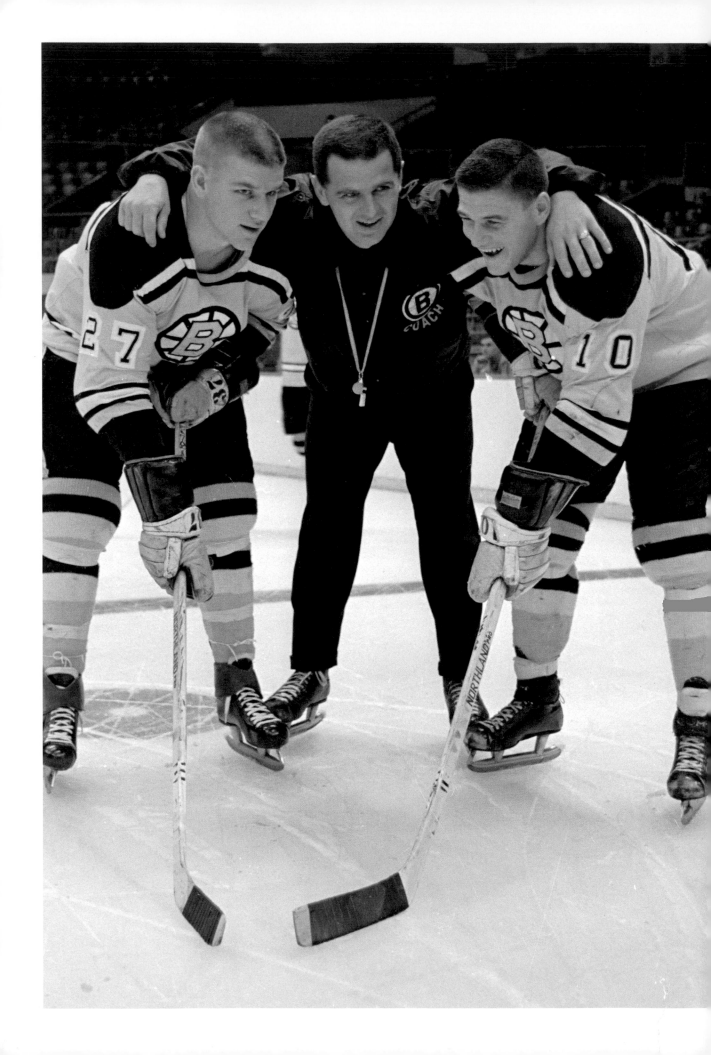

Harry Sinden COACH

When he was named Bruins head coach in 1966, the 33-year-old Sinden was the youngest coach in the league, leading the league's youngest team. It didn't help matters that the Bruins were also among the league's worst clubs. But within four years, the fiery Sinden's demanding leadership style and eye for talent had the Bruins hoisting the Stanley Cup as league champions. Sinden left the team in 1970, but in 1972, he became the Bruins' general manager, a post he held until 2000. Sinden's dedication to the team also compelled him to serve two more short stints as the team's coach.

BRUINS SEASONS AS COACH: 1966–70, 1979–80, 1984–85
NHL COACHING RECORD: 151–121–58
STANLEY CUP CHAMPIONSHIP WITH BOSTON: 1970
HOCKEY HALL OF FAME INDUCTEE (1983)

BRUINS

INDEX

A

Art Ross Trophy 8, 10, 26

B

Bauer, Bobby 10, 44
Bergeron, Patrice 42
Boston Garden 5, 13, 18
Bourque, Ray 32, 34, 36, 37, 38, 40
Brimsek, Frank 12
Bucyk, Johnny 16, 18, 20, 37

C

Calder Trophy 12, 20, 22, 28, 32, 34
Cashman, Wayne 20, 22
Chara, Zdeno 42
Cheevers, Gerry 22, 25
Cherry, Don 28, 30
Chiarelli, Peter 42
Clapper, Aubrey "Dit" 10, 37
Cowley, Bill 14

D

Dafoe, Byron 38
Doak, Gary 10
Dumart, Woody 10
"Dynamite Line" 10

E

Esposito, Phil 10, 22, 24, 26, 37

F

first season 8
FleetCenter 13

G

Gainor, Norman "Dutch" 10
Guidolin, Armand "Bep" 31

H

Hart Trophy 10, 14, 26, 28
Hitchman, Lionel 37
Hockey Hall of Fame 10, 16, 25, 28, 34, 40
Hodge, Ken 18, 22

K

Knuble, Mike 40

L

LaBine, Leo 16
Lady Byng Trophy 16
Lemelin, Reggie 36

M

Mackell, Fleming 16
Marcotte, Don 22
Middleton, Rick 28
Milbury, Mike 28
Moog, Andy 32, 36
Murray, Glen 40

N

National Hockey League records 14, 16, 24, 25, 28, 30, 34
Neely, Cam 34, 36, 37
Norris Trophy 28, 34

O

Oliver, Harry 8
O'Ree, Willie 19
O'Reilly, Terry 22, 28, 34, 37
Orr, Bobby 5, 20, 22, 24, 26, 28, 32, 37

P

Park, Brad 26, 28
Pederson, Barry 34

Peirson, John 16
playoffs 5, 10, 12, 14, 16, 22, 24, 30, 34, 36, 40, 42
Primeau, Wayne 42

R

Ratelle, Jean 26, 28
retired sweaters 22, 37
Ross, Art 8

S

Samsonov, Sergei 38
Sanderson, Derek 22, 24
Savard, Marc 42
Schmidt, Milt 10, 37
Shore, Eddie 8, 10, 14, 32, 37
Sinden, Harry 47
Stanley Cup championships 5, 10, 12, 13, 14, 24, 25, 44, 47
Stanley Cup Finals 5, 13, 14, 16, 22, 24, 30, 34, 36
Stuart, Brad 42
Sturm, Marco 42

T

TD Banknorth Garden 13, 37
team fight song 45
team name 8
team records 18
Thompson, Cecil "Tiny" 12, 40
Thornton, Joe 34, 38, 40, 42

V

Vezina Trophy 12, 40

W

Weiland, Ralph "Cooney" 10

BRUINS